Three Things

That *Everybody*

Wants To **Know**

About **You**

The **Five** Step Plan

For **Life Success**

Ernst Fenelon Jr

ISBN: 978-1-7322745-0-1 (Paperback)

Library of Congress Control Number: 2018904959

Front cover art work by Jeremiah Fenelon.
Book design by Ernst Fenelon Jr.

Printed by DiggyPOD, Inc., in the United States of America.

First printing edition 2018.

Published by Ernst Fenelon Jr.
For more information, visit www.ernstfenelonjr.com

DEDICATION

This book is dedicated to my Son,
Jeremiah. May this book guide you one day
to fulfill every dream your heart truly
desires.

ACKNOWLEDGMENTS

There are so many people to thank for the wisdom, guidance, and inspiration in creating this book. If I were to thank them all, that would be a book in itself! Even if I tried, inevitably I would leave someone out. However, I would feel remiss if I didn't thank several people by name who are significant individuals in my life who supported me in completing this book.

First I want to thank Allah, Almighty God, The Most High, for more blessings than I can count and for the grace to complete this book. Like in the book and life, my faith is my grounding point and my bedrock.

I thank my mom, Marie Ange Fenelon, for inspiring me to make my Faith foremost and central in life. She's been with me from my first breath, through the valleys and peaks of my life journey, all without fail or falter. Her ability to be positive, loving and resilient no matter what life throws at her truly amazes me and has given me an amazing example and role model. Her ability to encourage me to be the best version of myself has meant the world and all that's in it! She's the wind beneath my wings!

I thank my wife, Lori, who has been by my side for the last 11 years (10 years married), through a lot of rainy days and plenty of sunshine. Her support has been critical as I have pursued many adventures of significance, especially becoming a published author. She is the fun, spontaneous "Yin" to my rigidly structured "Yang." As I tend to the pruning of the rose bush of life, she reminds me to stop and take the time to smell the flowers. She is my fierce ally when the world pushes my back against the wall. She holds down the home when I'm off in service to the world and is such an incredible mom to our rambunctious five-year-old, Jeremiah. I'm grateful for all that she does and that she took a chance on me. She is the Love of my Life.

I thank my friend and mentor for over a dozen years, Dr. Renford Reese. He is the big brother I never had. A big part of actually writing this book was his constant encouragement about the potential value I, and the book could bring to others. His ability to see me as I could be and not who I have been inspired me to challenge myself and grow in ways unimaginable. His unwavering support and belief in my abilities dispel any doubts of my own. I profoundly appreciate, to the depths of my soul, his readiness to have my back and create opportunities for me to gain and flourish. His loyalty to me and my wellbeing is unique and profound. He has changed my life and hopefully will continue to do so for many years to come.

I thank my best friend in the world, Eric Ferguson. 30+ years of friendship, for his motivating support! One of the few human beings on the planet that I have never gotten into an argument with, regardless of agreement or not. Born on the same day (different year), we clicked like we were two peas in a pod from day one. His shoulders are the broad ones I have leaned on in tragedy and hoisted upon in triumph. We have shed tears of laughter and tears of sorrow. He is definitely one of my six (you'll understand after reading the book).

I thank my friend Ayesha Waraich, who transcribed, edited and was a phenomenal resource for feedback and clarity! Her dedication to seeing this book done while studying for the LSAT, working, volunteering with the Prison Education Project and other organizations, applying to law schools and having a life will remain forever priceless! Her ability to adapt to changes and challenges of technology and a first-time author who didn't have a clue what he was doing is an excellent indication of her future success based on flexibility and mental agility.

I thank Elizabeth Goldhammer for being the tremendous chief proofreader for this book! I much appreciated your time, energy, guidance and input to make this book so much better than when you received it!

I thank Stephanie Gergeres for interviewing me for her internet magazine, *Juicy Highlights.* You are a skillful reporter who asked thought-provoking questions which caused me to reflect deeply on my incredible life journey so far. The interview (included in this book) is the blueprint for my story and my evidence that I have done the "work" of which I write. I often read it all over again as a great reminder and for course correction.

I thank Raabia Waraich for her constant positive support in creating this book. Your feedback was valuable and appreciated.

A Final "thank you" to all of the friends and family who sent support and love, through social media or direct contact, while I endeavored to create something beneficial to many.

Table of Contents

PREFACE i

Why Did I Write This Book? i

INTRODUCTION 1

Who is This Book For? 1

What are The Three Questions? 2

What is the Five Step Plan
for Life Success? 2

Chapter 1:Have You
Connected the Dots? 4

Our Beliefs....................................6

The "F" Word (No, Not That One!) 10

Temporary External Change Versus

Permanent Internal Transformation.......12

Moving From Reacting to Responding....14

Chapter 2: Have You
Invested in Yourself? 17

Using Education as Evidence...............18

Environment versus Will 19

Actions + Behavior = Character 20

Chapter 3: What Value Do
You Bring to the Table.....................24

Would You Buy You? 27

Chapter4: Five Step
Plan for Life Success 28

Planning and Defining Life Success.........29

Chapter 5: Dreams (Step 1).........................34

The First F - Faith 37

The Second F - Family/Friends 38

The Third F - Finance 42

The Fourth F - Fitness...............................46

The Fifth F - Fun 48

The First C - Local Community...............49

The Second C - Global Community.........52

Chapter 6: Goals (Step 2) 54

S.M.A.R.T. Goals.......................................55

Impossible Versus Improbable.................56

Chapter 7: The Plan (Step 3).....................59

Blending Goals into a Plan 60

Inflexible Outcome, Flexible Approach...62

Chapter 8: Schedule (Step 4).....................65

Twenty-Four Hours in a Day 65

Scheduling Everything...............................69

Crystal Balls versus Rubber Balls 71

Chapter 9: Accountability (Step 5)..............72

Accountability: Self or Coach? 72

Impact of Environment,.............................76

Internal & External Influences 76

Chapter 10: The Secret Ingredient 83

Chapter 11: The Interview 87

I Had Lost Faith, As My
Life Turned Out Differently
Than I Expected....................................88

18 Great Reads on Transformation
of Mindset and Soul.............................101

About the Author...................................102

PREFACE

Why Did I Write This Book?

"If you can change the way you look at things, the things you look at change."
- **Wayne Dyer**

This book was born from the encouragement of countless people that my life story is one that can inspire belief in the power of transformation. My life has gone from living the American Dream to experiencing the devastating loss of it. In the process, I became an alcoholic, suicidal, hurt person who hurt people. I almost lost my life in the process of a series of tragic choices 27 years ago. It was at near death I began the process of transformation to a life of love, contribution, sobriety, hope, passion, and fulfillment. I found purpose and passion for life again. What were some of the tools I used to make that compelling Transformation? It's in this book!

The contents of this book came from a mixture of fifty years of self-reflection, thousands of hours of personal development, and the life plan that has given me fulfillment. The greatest boxer of all time, Muhammad Ali, once said, "The man who views the world at 50 the same as he did at 20 has wasted 30 years of his life." At 51 years on earth, my thinking and behavior are vastly different than when I was in my 20's. How I deal with "failures" (I share my perspective about the other "F" word) later. How I walk, talk, eat, drink and move are very different in a positive way. During the past 30 years, I have embraced the concept that life is about the responsibility of choices we make and the accountability of the consequences that follow. I began to study successful people and learn the critical difference between reacting and responding. I define reacting as taking action without forethought to the consequences. I define responding as thinking, at the speed of thought, about the consequential effects of whatever action one may do, will have on what one values most and choosing accordingly. The idea that constant and repetitive focus on one's dreams, goals, values, and needs can help one respond rather than react, selecting favorable consequences in almost any situation, really resonated with me. As I became more precise about my dreams and goals, the positive implications of many of my decisions reflected the clarity of my focus.

For the record, I am not professing that I am perfect or have all the answers. I'm not, and I don't. I still make errors and mistakes, just like everyone else. However, when I do get "off course" in pursuit of my dreams, the system I am sharing has provided the necessary constant "course correction" to regain crystal clarity of my deepest values so I can make the best choices towards achieving my "life success." My aim with this book is to help guide you to achieve your life success according to your definition.

The five steps and the "five Fs (faith, family, finance, fitness, and fun)" concept came from the hundreds of hours of personal development classes, seminars, teleconferences, books and other events in which I participated. The five steps/five F's concept is not new. There is the common saying, "There is nothing new under the Sun" (Ecclesiastes 1:9). This saying applies to the five steps and five Fs concepts here. These tried and tested concepts have withstood the test of time. They are consistently used or modified in one way or another by most of the presenters of personal development I've listened to or met. I, in turn, have given my modified definition to the five F's and added the "Two Cs," creating an original take on the subject.

I developed the three questions concept over the past three decades from my personal experiences and conversations with incarcerated individuals from California in the USA to Uganda, Africa.

As the Senior Program Coordinator of the Prison Education Project (herein PEP), and an Instructor of the Leadership and Entrepreneur Courses, I created a curriculum based on the five steps, Five Fs, Two Cs and three questions. I wanted incarcerated students to have access to this information so they could have the tools to make better decisions about their lives and live a life of positive contribution and fulfillment.

I discovered as I talked to people from all walks of life about the concepts of the three questions everybody wants to know about you and the five step plan for life success, almost everyone said they could benefit from my wealth of information and insight into them. Ultimately, that is why I wrote this book: to benefit and inspire as many people as possible to transform their lives and help change the world one life at a time.

I do recognize that there are many people in situations which cannot be resolved with just positive thinking or just imagining the life that one wishes. They are not in control of their circumstances. However, even in the most oppressive and dangerous conditions, one's perspective can dramatically shape their experience of these conditions.

One great example of what I am talking about is Victor Frankl. He experienced the horror of the Holocaust and survived. He is quoted to have said, **"Everything can be taken from a man but one thing: the last of the human freedoms - to choose one's attitude in any given set of circumstances, to choose one's own way."** His perspective of the conditions was different than many and may have contributed to his survival. The one aspect of your perspective you can control is your attitude.

Hopefully, the value you will get from this book (through answering the three questions, defining your Five Fs and Two Cs and creating your own Life Success Plan) will be in being able to self-assess where you are in life, regarding happiness and contentment, and how you got there. If you are not happy and content, I wholeheartedly believe you can get some ideas from this book of what you can do about it.

My other desire is you'll be able to reflect and apply these questions to your life and achieve more fulfillment than you had before reading it! There are two things I've come to learn. One thing is that people know what they don't want, but very few people know what they do want. The other thing is people desire without specificity. I challenge you to be very specific in talking to the universe or anybody about precisely what is it that you do want.

This book was written for people who were just like me -Someone wanting to know what their actual values are and desiring a "blueprint" to build the life that they only imagine in their dreams.

At the end of the day, this book is all about you, your life and the possible discovery of untapped potential waiting for delivery into the world!

Let the discovery begin!

INTRODUCTION

Who is This Book For?

This book is not for everybody. This book is for anyone who is:

- Wanting to assess where they are in living the life they want according to their values and needs.
- Desiring crystal clarity as to what is crucial.
- Accepting that the transformational processes in this book are a way to get to the life they want.
- Feeling stuck in their career or job.
- At "a fork in the road' in life, but unclear how to make the major decision in front of them.
- Starting over from a life that has suddenly crumbled and they need help getting clarity what is next by defining what's important.
- Currently incarcerated. The work of transformation begins while inside the jail/prison, not when they get out. This book can help them create a blueprint for a transformational shift.
- Formerly incarcerated, especially if they've been out for a while and struggle to make the transition back into society.

Now you are probably asking some of the following questions: What are the three things everybody wants to know? What is the five step plan for life success? Inquiring minds want to know!

What are The Three Questions?

The three questions are:

1. Have you connected the dots (learned from the lessons that life offers you)?
2. Have you invested in yourself?
3. What value do you bring to the table?

What is the Five Step Plan for Life Success?

The five steps of the Life Success Plan are:

1. Dreams
2. Goals
3. Plan
4. Schedule
5. Accountability

If you already have the answers to the Three Questions and the Five Step of the Life Success Plan, then you don't have to read the book! Just close it, hand it off to somebody else or use it as a paperweight! But, if you want to delve deeper into the Three Questions and the Five Step of the Life Success Plan, then I invite you to continue to read this book.

I encourage you to get and use a bound notebook while reading this book to be able to write down any notes and the answers to questions at the end of the chapters. The "College" notebooks (durable cardboard cover and backing, sewn-bound pages, wide-lined paper, a label on the cover, etc.) are great for this purpose and inexpensive! They are stackable too should you need to use more than one!

The answers to the Three Questions and the Five Step of the Life Success Plan, when blended and written into a Life Success Plan, can lead you to live a life that is successful on your terms and experience a level of incomparable personal fulfillment!

Chapter 1
Have You Connected the Dots?

"Though nobody can go back and make a new beginning… Anyone can start over and make a new ending."
-Chico Xavier

Have you connected the "dots" of the moments of your life and learned from those lessons that life has offered you? I believe (and hope you would agree with) the following:

- The quality of life we live is seriously affected by the choices we make.
- The quality of the choices we make is directly impacted by the quality of the questions we ask ourselves.
- The quality of the questions we ask ourselves will depend considerably on our perspective and awareness of choices.

Many say, "Education is liberation," yet many "educated" people are far from being liberated. An "educated fool" is one who has book knowledge but lacks common sense or the ability to make necessary life decisions to their benefit. Educated fools may have a degree, but display various forms of ignorance such as racism.

So education in itself is not liberation. If education does not increase your awareness of the choices you have in life, is it really education? Education becomes liberation when it raises your awareness of more opportunities and choices you can make.

I often tell my son when he makes a poor choice that "experience is the best teacher." We all make poor choices from time to time. Like my son, sometimes we can't learn or appreciate good advice until we make a poor choice and deal with the accountability of the consequences. The education is liberation key can only set us free if we choose differently and more wisely the next time the opportunity (or life lesson) repeats itself. These teachable moments become the "dots" that make up our lives.

When you think of a picture where you have to connect the dots, you start from one point and, as you connect the dots, eventually an image or design appears. Similarly, if you were to connect the "dots" of your life, which are significant memory points and experiences, and it presented the picture of your life today, would you be satisfied with it? If you aren't, do you first understand how you got to this point? If you don't comprehend how you got to where you are today, then you won't grasp how you can change it. To know how you arrived at where you are currently, the questions you have to ask yourself are:

- What did you learn from each of the experiences the dots represent?
- Have you applied the principles of the lessons?
- Can you now take away a different lesson and apply it?
- Can you see different choices you can make?

Our Beliefs

So why do we make the choices we do? I believe our beliefs influence our thoughts, our thoughts influence our emotions, our emotions influence our choices of actions, and then our actions are the producers of our results. So ultimately our beliefs have a direct influence on the decisions we make and the results we get in life. If you believe you will be successful in life, then the way you approach opportunities or learn lessons will be different than if you think you will fail.

The next question you should honestly ask yourself is, do your beliefs get you closer to or further away from your most important dreams and goals? If your beliefs are not serving you to get closer to your ultimate dreams, how do you go about changing your beliefs? Let's discuss that in-depth.

There's a concept that says that environment can be stronger than will. What I have concluded is that environment is not just external; it is also internal. As you examine your beliefs about yourself and the world, some great questions to ask yourself are:

- What have been your internal influences and beliefs that have impacted your thoughts about yourself, the opportunities around you and the world in general?
- Who or what are your external influences, both positive and negative?

One of the fundamental principles of changing what you believe is that **you do not have to accept everything that was said to you about you**. Just because someone said something about you that has had a negative impact on you does not mean you have to believe or continue to believe that statement. For example, if someone told you, "you'll never amount to anything, you'll always get in trouble, you'll always fail, etc." You don't have to continue to hold on to those beliefs or any other if they are not getting you closer to your dreams and goals. However, beliefs that serve you (like

7

you can be anything you want to be or anyone you want to be) are ones you want to hold on to because they will serve you as you pursue your ultimate dreams.

A fundamental concept you have to realize is that, as Tony Robbins has said, "**Nothing has meaning other than what you give it**." When you think of any circumstance that occurred in your life, it only has the meaning that you've given it. As you look at each of the dots that make up your life thus far, and the purpose that you've given each of those dots, is it possible to shift what each of those dots means to you?

Someone asked me, "what if you don't achieve your ultimate dreams?" I answered, "Since I don't know when I'm going to die, I do my best to live focused on pursuing my most important dreams and growing into being who I need to be to fulfill them." The person you will become in pursuit of your dreams and goals will be vastly different from the person you were before pursuing them.

Most people think the pinnacle of life is achieving your ultimate goals and dreams. But it's not. The ultimate pinnacle of life is taking the transformation journey and becoming the best version of yourself. If in this process (journey), I don't achieve my ultimate dreams (destination), I will be more fulfilled than if I did not take the journey of transformation in the first place.

Life is best when lived by enjoying the journey, as you travel from destination to destination. One big mistake most people make is that they think life is only about the destinations. You graduate high school—that's a destination. You graduate college, you get married, you have children, you start a business, etc. These are all destinations too. But people believe these destinations are what life is all about. I would like to challenge that theory by stating that life is a journey, not a destination. All of those destinations are the dots that make up your life. They are part of the process.

Living life fully is a process, not an event. Imagine living a life in pursuit of what's important to you every moment and not what's important to somebody else. As you reflect on the dots of your life, what have you learned about the choices that you've made that have brought you to the point that you're at now? Have you made decisions that serve you?

Insanity is doing the same thing over and over again and expecting a different result. If you're not getting the results you want, I invite you to take a look and see if you're doing the same things over and over again. Maybe it doesn't look the same way, but it's the same thing in a new way. If you want to change what you're getting, you have to change what you're doing.

I said earlier that experience could be the best teacher. You can learn from two different levels of experience. You can learn from your own experiences, which is by trial and error. You do something, it doesn't work the way you wanted it to, and you choose not to do it again, or you choose to do it another way. That can only happen if you're clear on what your beliefs and desired results are, which affect actions and your actual results. Another way you can learn is from the experience of others.

The "F" Word (No, Not That One!)

Earlier I mentioned the word "failure." The dreaded "F" word. What is your definition of failure? Remember, nothing has a meaning other than what we give it. Your definition of failure is a crucial component to how you choose the opportunities that are in front of you because life is about choices. Most people define failure as not succeeding in whatever endeavor they chose to do or pursue. However, I would challenge you to look at failure through another lens. Failure is purely life's lessons in disguise.

Look at failure as part of the process to success. For example, if you have a batting average of .300 in baseball, your performance is considered astonishing! This percentage means that only one out of three times that you get up to bat, you actually get on base! So is that failure or is that success? In baseball terms, that's success.

If you view failure as a learning process rather than a final event, then you can learn and grow from each of the lessons that it gives you. Try asking yourself what the failure has taught you. Some people would look at Bill Gates when he dropped out of college and thought he was a failure. They would probably look at Albert Einstein, who was not considered very intellectual in eighth grade, the same way. They would perceive these two examples as failures at the moments they did not have "success." However, those individuals took those moments of what appeared to be a failure and turned them into opportunities for some of the most celebrated success stories in human history that we continue to talk about today.

Temporary External Change
Versus
Permanent Internal Transformation

The next area you need to look at regarding connecting the dots is temporary external change versus permanent internal transformation. My definition of what I believe the transient nature of change is any of us can get sick and tired of a situation or circumstance and change them immediately in the heat of the moment. Too frequently, that kind of changes doesn't last. Why? Because until we get utterly sick and tired of being sick and tired, and make internal transformations, they don't last. So why is the nature of change sometimes so temporary? Human nature is prone to return to our "comfort zone," even when our comfort zone does not serve us to get closer to our dreams. Therefore, once we get back in our comfort zone (which is where the situation we made the change began from), we just become comfortable with that same situation again.

On the other hand, transformation is when something becomes forever changed. Let's take a look at the caterpillar as an example of transformational change. There's a point in its life where the caterpillar goes into a cocoon. While inside the cocoon, the caterpillar goes through a metamorphosis. It

12

transforms into another creature; a beautiful butterfly! When it comes out of the cocoon, it's an entirely different creature; the way it functions is not the same. The way it breathes, moves, eats, and flies. Even when it dies, it will not go back to being a caterpillar.

In the same way, human beings need to transform if they want to get different results. How do we transform? Externally, we may look the same, but it is how we internally transform that counts. At the end of the day, either we're growing or dying. Either we're learning or forgetting. If we can take the lessons that are there for us to learn, then we can improve, transform and become better than we were yesterday. Ultimately, that's what people want to know from anyone who has ever made any mistakes or done anything which they have regretted, which makes up everybody on the planet! Most people want to know if you can learn from your mistakes, errors in judgment or your learned behavior dysfunctions. Now that you look at the dots that make up your life, do you have a better insight as to how you are where you are in life?

Every opportunity and experience you have in life is another opportunity to assess and learn from it. My question that I always ask myself no matter what happens, even things that I seemingly have no responsibility for, is "What can I learn from this?" If somebody who I don't know comes up to me and is irate, I ask myself, "What can I learn from this?"

Life is about learning, from the cradle to the grave. Look at every opportunity, even the occasions where someone has done injustice towards you, and ask what you can learn from that situation. Because if you can learn from every situation, then that can give you an opportunity for dramatic growth and awareness. The first step of transformation is awareness.

Moving From Reacting to Responding

One of the most important aspects of growth is shifting from reacting to responding. What is the difference? Reaction is just an automatic process of your nervous system. For example, if a ball is coming directly at you, you move out of the way without even thinking about it. Or it could be an emotional reaction. For example, if someone says a word, phrase or there's a tone in their voice, it can cause you to get upset.

I believe that response is different. Response is the process of thinking and deciding which actions you want to take based on what is important to you. One of the advantages that incarcerated people have over others is that they potentially have time to think. They have time to reflect on their lives and the results they have gotten. If they don't like the results they have obtained, they have an opportunity to learn how to respond. It's not always easy, but if they can take the time while they are away from society to learn how to respond, then there's an opportunity for tremendous growth. The question is: what do you think about during the process from when something happens to you to when you choose your response?

A critical technique in the process of growth is "peeling the onion." An onion has many layers before you get all the way down to the bulb of the onion. In the same way, the goal of peeling the onion is to deconstruct (peel back) your choices and to discover the reasoning, logic, and emotions behind them (bulb). When you've made bad choices or decisions, you should deconstruct why they occurred. Why do you react the way that you do? Why do you think the way that you do? Why do you behave the way that you do? In each of those areas, peeling the onion can give you tremendous insight into the root of your beliefs in each of those areas. Once you do, then you can make a choice and decide if that is going to give you the best results in life and, once again, direct you towards your life success. Ultimately, that is what is vital. If you don't learn how to reflect and choose what your response will be, you will forever be a prisoner of your reactions.

If you begin to deconstruct your current beliefs, how have they impacted your satisfaction or dissatisfaction with your life right now? Take a moment to write down your answer.

Chapter 2
Have You Invested in Yourself?

"The best investment you can make is in yourself."
-**Warren Buffet**

The most considerable investment you can make is knowing yourself and your motivations. One of the most important questions you can ask yourself is "What is the character of the person who achieves the dreams I have?" Most people spend too much of their time invested in knowing about things that do not serve them to live a passionately fulfilled life. They want to be distracted by watching daytime shows filled with relationship drama or at night time shows to learn more gossip about the current spotlight celebrities. What is it that they want to be distracted from? They want to be distracted from doing the uncomfortable work of growth. Life can be messy working with different emotions, feelings, and traumas. However, that is where success lies. Successful people learn to be comfortable with the uncomfortable work of self-growth. If you have connected the dots and learned from the lessons they provided you, what is the evidence that you've done the uncomfortable task of self-growth?

Using Education as Evidence

One of the areas is in education. Education, specifically academic education, is one area where you can evidence growth. Getting a GED, an A.A., B.A., Masters or a Ph.D. are evidence that you have invested in yourself. Degrees and certificates tell people that you committed to a course of action and completed it. Whatever obstacles or challenges came your way, you saw the process through until the end, and that says a lot about you. Many people don't complete college. Does that mean that those who get certificates or degrees are the only people qualified to be hired in a particular field? No, that's not what it means. However, it gives greater initial deference to their ability to do so.

Another way to evidence growth is through participating in self-help groups. Self-help groups are crucial because they can teach you coping mechanisms for emotional self-management, which can lead to greater self-awareness.

Environment versus Will

Your environment can be stronger than your will. Will or willpower can be defined as "control deliberately exerted to do something or to restrain one's impulses." Just because you've learned a lesson doesn't mean you apply it.

For example, most people at the end of the year make a New Year's resolution to improve their health and sign up for the gym. During January and February, people pack the gyms determined to change their lives and get into shape! By the time March comes around, you notice that there are fewer people than in January and there are lots of empty parking spaces! Why is that? Those individuals who stop going to the gym, even though they found themselves in a positive environment that could help them achieve their fitness goals, may not have had a strong will to keep going. Their will probably wasn't firmly connected to their "why" they should continue. Even though they were in the gym, they were also in other "environments," some of which were negative. Those could include self-doubt or internalizing criticism. If all of your environments are conducive to your growth, and you have a will strongly connected to your "why" to transform, then there is a high likelihood that you will do it and continue to do it.

19

Another way to grow comes from associations with others, both living and deceased.

You grow the most when you associate with people who are more knowledgeable by the application of knowledge than you, whether it may be in academics, spiritual, physical, mental or emotional growth. Seek associations that will challenge, stretch, or help you to develop to a higher capacity to transform. All of us have more levels for us to reach within our lives.

You can also associate with the deceased. Right now, you're probably asking, "Why in the world would I want to associate with the dead?" Many of those who have passed on have left books or CDs that many people benefit from today. Hopefully someday when I've passed on, people will benefit from this book as well.

Actions + Behavior = Character

If you are unable to speak about your transformation or your growth, what would your actions say? Would they demonstrate and provide evidence that you've changed? Or would your actions speak volumes about how much you haven't changed or only changed on the surface? You want to begin to take a closer look at your actions and behaviors.

20

Right now, look in the mirror and ask yourself this question: is there actually evidence in your actions and behaviors that you've grown? If there is proof, great. But if there isn't, then go back and look at the bulb (peeling the onion) of your repeating patterns of behavior. Behavior is the clearest evidence of transformation.

A definition of "character" is your essential qualities exhibited by your repeated patterns of behavior. Repeated actions become habits. Repeated habits become your behavior. Repetitive behaviors become your character. If you want to shift your character, then you would have to change your actions and behaviors. Are your current activities and behaviors getting you closer or further from the character you need to have to achieve your goals? Some questions you should ask yourself are:

- What is controlling your actions?
- Can your actions be controlled by words or the actions of others?
- Are your actions an impulsive reaction to your emotions?

The most important factor to remember about your
actions is that when emotions are high, intelligence (ability to
think and process) is low. When intelligence is high, feelings
are low. The critical component you need to ask yourself at
any given moment is what is controlling you. Is it your
emotions or is it your intelligence? Or is it a blend of the two,
which is where you want to be.

One of the most effective tools you can use in the
process of growth and controlling potential negative
influences is learning a tactic called "nip it in the bud." It
means to stop something before it becomes ingrained or
problematic. If you have habits that are counterproductive or
destructive towards accomplishing your dreams, where you
want to go in life, and the character you want to have, then
your number one task is to "nip it in the bud." You want to
begin paying attention to your habits of how you talk, think,
behave and react. If you see a harmful pattern start to take
hold, nip it in the bud and replace it with patterns of behavior
that serve you. Don't just stop doing a bad habit because it
will more than likely reoccur or remerge, potentially in a
different form if you do not replace it with a good one. You
have to replace it with something because you cannot just stop
it from potentially resurfacing. Replacing bad habits with

good ones is one tool you can use to further evidence your own personal internal and external growth.

Take a moment and write down the answer to these questions:

- What is the evidence that you have invested in your personal growth, both internally and externally?
- Who are your associations, living and/or deceased?
- Write down several traits of what you believe is your character.
- Name three behaviors you want to work on to change and with what behaviors would you replace them.

Chapter 3

What Value Do You Bring to the Table?

"You don't get paid by the hour. You get paid for the value you bring to the hour."
-Jim Rohn

Value has many meanings, but it will be defined here as:

- Being beneficial to others.
- Adding substance or significance.
- One's judgment of what is paramount.

The blessings in life (spiritual joy, meaningful relationships, financial success, robust health, etc.) are the by-product of the value you bring.

After people have accepted the fact that you can connect the dots that make up your life and that you have invested in your growth, the next thing they want to know is what value do you bring to the table? I want to invite you to ask yourself, do you bring value to the tables in your life (whether it is in a personal, business or social relationship)? For example, if you're seeking financial success, money is the byproduct of the value you bring to people, whether it is from selling a product or providing a service.

Imagine that you're having a dinner, get-together or potluck where everyone has contributed, and an individual shows up with no contribution and doesn't help and says, "Can I participate?" How would you feel and the others who contributed feel? When someone doesn't contribute and doesn't bring any value to the table, they take away value. How much more dynamic and valuable would their presence be if they came and said, "Hey, I'm bringing (_____)" "I'm willing to help (_____)." Strive to be the latter example and not the former one.

Other questions you can ask yourself are:
- In what way can you volunteer?
- In what way can you aid a situation?
- In what way can you bring your life experience to the situation to benefit others?

Ultimately, that is how we add value; by giving our time, energy and focus. Sometimes the highest value we can provide is just smiling and acknowledging another person's existence.

When it comes to adding value to a business, please do your research. If you're going to be a part of the business, you should learn about the business. You need to know who its competitors are and what ways you can personally add to the growth of the company. In a job interview, they're going to want to know two things from you: how are you going to make the business money and save the business money? If you can clearly and decisively answer these two questions, your chances of being hired are greatly enhanced.

Keep in mind that creating value may not mean you will immediately get monetary value right away. One of the best ways to create value for yourself and your community is to volunteer. Once you create value, opportunities will begin to flow your way! When people see you show up and give of your whole self, then they may consider you for other opportunities. For example, when the next job opportunity comes up, they may say, "Hey, I like how that person volunteers, how they come in early, stay late and have a good attitude." Therefore, look for opportunities to give and create value through volunteering.

Would You Buy You?

Imagine if you were a product: would you buy you? Why would you buy you? It sounds silly but think about it. Why do you buy the products (car, home, washing machine, coffee maker, food, etc.) or services (realtor, lawyer, tailor, etc.) that you do? You buy them because you find value in them! So if you were on the shelf, would you buy you? What would be the advertisement for the value you bring? What are the key features and benefits of associating, hiring, working with and being around you? If your "competition" were to point out the less desirable qualities of your product, what would they say? Being self-aware of those factors is critical because they give you the opportunity to grow. Take a moment to write down a few sentences answering the following questions:

- What value do you bring to each of your tables (personal, social, business)?
- In what ways can you bring more value?
- If you are not clear about the value you bring to your tables, then ask others you respect what value you bring.

Chapter 4
Five Step Plan for Life Success

"Three simple rules in life: If you do not go after what you want, you'll never have it. If you do not ask, the answer will always be no. If you do not step forward, you will always be in the same place."
-Anonymous

A life success plan is the "blueprint" for your life. If you were to build a house, the first thing you have to do is have an idea what it's going to look like (your life dreams). Then, you have to come up with the specifics (your life goals). Now, you're going to create a blueprint (your life success plan) to put it all together.

The five steps to a dynamic Life Success Plan are:

1. Dreams
2. Goals
3. Plan
4. Schedule
5. Accountability

These five steps, if taken together, can lead you to live a life that is successful on your terms.

Planning and Defining Life Success

Why plan for life success? If you fail to plan (for success), then you plan to fail. Either way, you are planning so you might as well prepare for success! How do you define success, especially when it comes to your life? People have described success as being number one. Others have defined it as not only being excellent, but nearly perfect, etc. Those are definitions of success that may not be possible all the time. One way to define success is to consistently live your life on your terms, doing the things you want to do, with the people you want to do them with and when you want to do them. Some people define success as being an entrepreneur. Others define success as being a great employee. Ultimately, success, in part, is just being grateful to be alive and appreciative of those around you because your circumstances can change dramatically in an instant.

Take a moment now and write down three or four ideas of what life success means to you. Be as specific as you can. Don't only say I want to be "rich" or "healthy." Define precisely what those terms mean to you. For one person, being rich might mean they want to be a millionaire, while someone else wants to be a billionaire.

There's a quote by Martin Luther King Jr. that says, "Most people die at 25, they just don't get buried until they're 65."

- What exactly does this quote mean?
- Why do most people die so young?
- Why is there a 40-year wait for burial?

The numbers are symbolic. 25 years old is symbolic for when we give up on our dreams. We're still young, but challenges to the life we dreamt of continue to happen. For some of us, we have to start paying back college debt, so we get any job, working in any field that may not even be related to our college degree. Some begin to have families and become focused on taking care of them. Others may develop a serious illness. Family members may require focused attention. Numerous challenges may come up that affect how people proceed with their lives. Slowly, those challenges push their dreams further and further to the back of their pursuits until they are 65 years old.

65 years old is symbolic because it represents the age of traditional retirement. There have been studies that show that those who retire (whether early or traditionally at 65 years old) who do not have an active social, physical and mental lifestyle have a higher risk of death in the first few

30

years after retirement than their counterparts who do have active lifestyles. Add in any regret of not pursuing one's dreams, and the quote seems to make more sense.

65 years old is also symbolic of when people pass away. What passes with them? Their unique dreams and goals! That book, song or dance never done. All of their dreams, goals, and adventures never happened. All of those great things never occurring!

Some say that in life you will regret the things you did not do. Since none of us are guaranteed tomorrow, my invitation to you is to recognize right now what you are passionate about and what it is that you genuinely want to do, and go do it!

Most people spend more time planning one single vacation then they do planning out their life in the areas of their faith, family, finances, fitness, and fun. Many unexpected changes can happen in life that can take you off course. How do you get back on track? Use a technique called "course correction." By consistently reviewing your life success plan, you get the chance to make "course corrections" to stay on track to accomplishing your goals.

When NASA launches a rocket, it is continuously veering off course, due to different forces affecting its trajectory. NASA readjusts the boosters thrust through calculated "course corrections" for the rocket to get to where it's meant to go.

Just like in your life, there are "forces" that are going to come up (different challenges, obstacles, setbacks, and circumstances) that will cause your life to go off course. There may be many demands from family, friends, work, social affairs, and social media. Pretty soon, if you are not careful, you may forget exactly where you were going. How will you know when to "course correct" if you don't have a life success plan?

For example, if you plan a vacation to drive from California to New York, you plan how much money you need, how much gas you may use, what vehicle you plan to travel in, where you'll be staying, and what sights you would see. You may have to adjust your schedule as different challenges come up to meet this plan.

Have you done that much planning for your life or do you magically expect the life you want just to happen? If you haven't done that much intricate planning, then this is an excellent opportunity for you to make a plan that is adjustable and flexible. Stay inflexible about your outcome, but flexible about your approach. Be flexible about your means, but not about your ends.

I hope as you read this book that you'll begin digging deep to discover what is truly important to you. Self-discovery of what your most treasured values are is where the Five Step Process will bring you the maximum value.

Chapter 5
Dreams (Step 1)

"A dream is a wish your heart makes, when you're fast asleep."
-Walt Disney Company, Cinderella

When we hear the word dreams, what does that even mean? For some people, they think of fantastical, outlandish, improbable types of circumstances. Other people think of their dream car, dream house, dream spouse or dream job. Some people think on more practical terms. At the end of the day, a dream is a wish your heart makes. A dream is something that inspires you, gives you goosebumps and gets you to do the improbable. A dream is something that captures the imagination and the heart at the same time. It is almost as if it is something the dreamer has been destined to be or do all along.

What are your dreams? What are the emotional ideas that reach out to you in the middle of the night, and you know that if you get them, it may be your life purpose or destiny? What notions touch you and make you believe they will make your life feel genuinely purposeful and complete? Have you defined them? Do you even know how they look, feel and sound? How explicit are they to you? Have you spent enough time implementing your dreams or have you allowed life to beat you down and get you further away from your dreams? For every dream you have, and for every dream you have allowed yourself to believe you cannot achieve, there is somebody out there with similar circumstances or worse who overcame different challenges and made their dreams come true. The question is: will you pursue your dreams at that level with everything you have and everything you can do? Ultimately, that is where life success lives. You may differ in opinion, but I believe it's in the doing, pursuing and being that makes a person a champion, not just in the title. Even I allowed life to push back my dream of being an author for many years. Then recently, I reassessed what my dreams were, took the first step, began to write and now you are reading my first book!

What is the first step on your journey? One of my favorite quotes is by Lao Tzu: *"The journey of a thousand miles begins with one step."* Have you taken the first step towards your dreams?

I invite you to take that first step and eventually a leap of faith. Often dreams are scary because when you consider that first step, you don't know what is going to happen. Success begins by just taking that first step. Sometimes you will not be number one of whatever your dream is. For example, let's say you want to make it to the Olympics. Is the dream really that you become number one in the world or is it getting to the Olympics, participating, doing your best and representing your country and your family? Either way, you need to take the first step! The power of dreams is something that can inspire you to go against logic, reason, culture, systems or everything rational to pursue something that captures your heart.

The first step of the first step is defining what exactly your dreams are. When people are defining their dreams, there seem to be several categories that are consistent. I call these categories the Five F's and Two C's. The Five F's are Faith, Family, Finance, Fitness, and Fun. The Two C's are your local community and the global community. Once you clearly define what is important to you in each of these categories, then they will determine what you need to focus on in the other steps of the life success plan.

The First F - Faith

The first F is faith. What is faith? Some would define faith as things that you hope for, but the evidence of those things are unseen. Some have belief in a higher power, a system or themselves. It is something that is innate in most human beings and something that pulls them forward and allows them to take bold steps.

Once you've defined your idea of faith, identify three areas of growth, improvement or transformation that you would like to see in this category. For example, if you believe in a higher power, there may be sacred sites that you wish to visit, books that you want to read, or you may want to spend more time in prayer or meditation.

Stop here and write down three growth goals regarding faith you desire to attain in the next 90 days.

The Second F – Family and Friends

The next F stands for family and friends. By definition, family can mean several things. There's the biological sense. There's also the community sense of family. One of my dear relatives says that some friends become family, but not all family becomes friends.

As you define who family is to you, I want to give you a scenario that will help sharpen the importance of that definition. Imagine, for no apparent reason and all of a sudden, you start having a very dry cough and start to feel ill. Within an hour, you have a raging fever. Nothing is making you feel better. You decide to see a doctor, and they give you the news that it is something they have never encountered before. It is spreading rapidly, and the doctor says you only have 24 to 48 hours to live. They will allow up to five people you care about to visit, comfort and spend time with you during those last moments. My question to you is who those five people would be? There may be many faces and names flashing before you right now. If you don't have five, then write down whoever you have, but the maximum number of people is five. Who would they be? So many people I love come to mind and I would want all of them in that room, but if I could only have five, I know who they would be. At the

38

end of the day, the other seven billion plus people on planet Earth do not matter more than these five people do to me in those fleeting moments. Those people represent my core family, and they are central to the fight for my dreams.

Who would your five people be? What would you want them to say about your relationship with them and their relationship with you? If you were to write your eulogy today, what would it say? Would you have done the things you wanted to do in this life? Would you have established the relationships with your loved ones the way you wanted to? Would you have said phrases like:

I'm sorry

I forgive you

I care about you

I love you

I was thinking about you

Or would you be that person who would be buried with all those sentiments still in their chest, heart, and mind when they die?

Often when people pass away, there are a lot of tears at funerals. One of the reasons I believe people shed tears is because of the things they didn't say or do for the person while they were alive and there was an opportunity to do so. I invite you to embrace the idea to nurture the five most important relationships to you now.

One of the most problematic challenges in life is that we often seek approval from other people, even for our very own existence. Some people seek approval from those who will never give it to them. Some of those people might be the people who are closest to you; it might even be the person who raised you. I invite you to realize that the most important person to get the approval of you, *is* you.

One of the awe-inspiring blessings in life I have experienced was the privilege to work in a hospice. I encountered several individuals who died, transitioning out of this life for the next. The movie *Ghost* seemed to capture what I imagine happened to them. There were two, starkly different experiences. Some people went so quietly that I didn't realize that they had passed on. Some even left with a smile on their face. Others, however, seemed to have departed in agony of regret. I share these sacred experiences because they had a profound effect on me. From that point forward, I have worked very hard not to be in the same position as those who seemed to have intense regret. I continue to work on making sure I say the "I love you's" and spend quality time with the people I care about most. Even though it is a driving force and a focus of mine to let them know they matter dearly to me, I fall short, as the hectic pace of modern life can be distracting. When I feel like that, I use "course correction" to renew my intention and immediately reach out to one of those people.

I invite you to become aware of who really matters to you and if you have even one person, count yourself blessed in a world that people seem to feel so lonely. Stop and write down the name(s) of your family.

The Third F - Finance

The third F is Finance. Evidence has shown that people who have won the lottery and received a lot of money tend to be financially broke, with their family life in chaos, within two years. Why is that the case? One reason may be the idea how you do small things is the way you are likely to do big things. If you mismanage a small amount of money, you are likely to mismanage a large amount of money. A lot of people say they want to be wealthy, but if people became billionaires overnight, would they be able to handle it? Or would they in a few years potentially become bankrupt, suicidal and have their family in disarray? Or would they be one of those who would manage their money in a way that would benefit them, everyone around them and the world at large?

My relationship with money all the way up until my 40's was one of scarcity. After my father (who was a doctor) became sick and was unable to sustain work, I watched all of the money he had earned disappear. We went from living the American dream to living the American nightmare. When my father passed away at 52, we had to file for bankruptcy. From that point on, I developed a fear that money would come and go rapidly and I would always be in a financially challenged

42

situation. I learned to have a spendthrift relationship with money. Often when the money arrived, I had no idea where I wanted it to go, but it always found a place. I've learned that they do not call money "currency" without reason. When you think of a current, it is always moving, and money is the same way. If you don't tell it where to go, it's going to find a place to go.

I found that I had to readjust my relationship with money if I was going to get over my fear and increase my net worth. I was fortunate to go to a seminar by T. Harv Eker called "The Secrets of the Millionaire Mind" where I realized many of my money issues stem from childhood. My present relationship with money isn't perfect, but I can say it has improved significantly because I have worked on how I manage a small amount of money in preparation for the more significant sums of money to come.

A couple of books that significantly helped me increase my financial acuity were *Rich Dad, Poor Dad* and *The Cashflow Quadrant*, both written by Robert Kiyosaki. I learned that I should have multiple streams of income, and they should be different types (active, passive, residual and royalty). I also learned how to make my money work for me instead of me working for money. I continue to grow in being an investor rather than just a wage earner. Investors benefit from knowing about compound interest and principles like the "rule of seventy-two," which is dividing 72 by an annual interest rate to know how long it will take for your money to double. Understanding how to make my money grow through automatic and manual savings programs has increased my knowledge of my net worth. The bottom line is not how much money someone makes, but how much money they keep, save and distribute it where they want it to go.

One of the wealth building steps I encourage everyone to do is get an estate plan. It's still amazing to me how many entertainers and pro athletes do not have an estate plan. Once they pass away, their estate goes into probate, and they lose much of their net worth, whether it's through a lot of taxation, a lot of fighting amongst family about the property, or a significant financial tragedy. So I encourage you to begin to learn how to protect all of your hard work by getting an estate plan.

What is your relationship with money? Is it something complex like rocket science or more like a game you enjoy? Once you understand the objective of the "money game" (that it is not something that controls you but, you control it), your relationship with money will become fun.

What are your financial goals? How much money do you want to make, and more importantly, save? By when? How are you going to do it? What do you want to pay off? Be clear, specific and very detailed about your financial goals. Stop and write down three specific financial goals.

The Fourth F - Fitness

The fourth "F" is Fitness. Fitness to me is synonymous with health. Health is a precious commodity that some of us are fortunate to have but many of us abuse. I'm paraphrasing the Dalai Lama when he said, "A person will sacrifice their health to seek wealth and then sacrifice their wealth to regain their health." Don't be that person! Apparently, none of us get out of this life alive. Ultimately, you have to ask yourself how you define the importance of health. I rate health high in my life because it gives me both the quality and quantity of life I want. When I have excellent health, life is great!

When I was in my early twenties, I was an alcoholic and became very ill. I wasn't exercising regularly, ate a lot of junk food, and got little sleep. I then contracted Hepatitis C through a blood transfusion. My body began to deteriorate.

I began to take lots of prescription medications. Pretty soon, I was taking between ten to fifteen pills a day. I took some pills to counteract the side effects of others. It wasn't until I got a severe medical warning about my health that I realized one area of my health that I had to get under control was my internal stress levels. My internal stress levels came from how I perceived things and the meaning I gave them. The combination of high internal stress levels, with poor

46

eating, sleep and exercise habits, caused my blood pressure to rise to the point of nearly stroke level. I had to make drastic changes. I began to exercise vigorously and regularly. I scrutinized what I ate and took into my body. My health began to improve. I started to reduce my medications until I didn't have to take any prescription medications for my physical, mental or emotional health by my 40th birthday. Still, to this day, I don't have to take any prescription medication! I am so grateful for where my health is today. My health and fitness are very vital to me, especially now that I have a five-year-old son who demands a lot of physical energy! I am grateful I have continued to exercise regularly to maintain a level of superb fitness.

Often people think health only means physical, but it should also include mental, emotional, psychological and spiritual health too. When we are healthy in all of these areas, then we have an excellent quality of life. What are your fitness goals? Stop and write down three specific fitness goals.

The Fifth F - Fun

The Last "F" is for fun. I'm defining fun as something that you do which you thoroughly enjoy, makes you laugh, have a great time and is not an obligation. It's probably one of the items you have on your "bucket list" (you do have one, don't you?). It is doing the things that make life more meaningful, worthwhile and juicy! I have lots of fun going to sci-fi movies, spending time with family and friends, reading personal development books, jet skiing and traveling.

What is your definition of fun? What would be the top three activities on your bucket list? If there were no limits, what would you do or where would you go? Take a moment and write down the top three fun activities that you really want to do that you currently aren't doing or haven't done. What would be the top three things that need to happen to start the journey towards doing them? Write those items down too! Now that you are clear on what top three things you want to do, what needs to happen to make them happen, all that's left is to take the first step and . . . have fun!

The First C - Local Community

Now that you have defined what is important to you personally in the categories of the Five F's, the next task is to identify what is important to others. One of the greatest things a human being can do is something for somebody else, particularly those who cannot do anything for them in return. The spiritual ideals of *do unto others as you would want them to do unto you* and *want for another as you would want for yourself* embody this behavior.

You may want to consider becoming a philanthropic entrepreneur. An entrepreneur is one who engages in activity to gain a profit. Philanthropic is giving or doing something because of one's love for humanity or the greater social good. So the philanthropic entrepreneur not only earns a profit to take care of themselves and their family but also for the betterment of the community around them. They think of the big picture of humanity. They tend to think about years, decades and generations to come. This codified philosophic principle is in the founding documents of the "Iroquois Confederacy," which states the Seven Generation Principle is that one should consider the impact of every decision on the next seven generations.

When you think of some of the great leaders, their greatness lies in their ability to be selfless in their endeavors to shape the world to become a better place. Whatever hardship was occurring (poverty, hunger, homelessness, racism, bigotry, violence, etc.), the first place they always started was within their immediate communities, and then their impact would grow. There is an internal value for some to contribute and become part of something bigger than themselves. For some, there is a higher reward in giving than receiving.

One of the catalysts of change in my life was when I was invited to do an extreme home makeover for a senior woman who could not take care of her property. Many different people showed up to volunteer. Some were professionals (carpenters, electricians, tile setters, etc.) and some, like me, were just regular citizens. Trucks came to uproot tree stumps and clear away wood. There was a dumpster for debris. By the time we finished, you could not recognize the property. The real reward was when it came time to see the senior woman's reaction. She was teary-eyed and had the most joyful smile from ear to ear. It was amazing to experience, and it compelled me to want to have that experience over and over again.

You may be asking: what can one person do? People don't care how much you know until they know how much you care. People in need don't care if you have a Ph.D. or GED; they only care if you are sincere in helping them. Volunteering is a tremendous opportunity to participate in activities that are already going on. Most nonprofits are in need of volunteers, staff, and money. I challenge you to not only to give money but also roll up your sleeves and get directly involved. There is something magical about direct involvement that shifts, changes and transforms the spirit.

Take a moment to consider your local community (the local community could be your household, neighbors, city or state) and begin to think of at least three ways you can contribute wherever you are to make it a little bit better. What is a social good you can do? Where can you volunteer? Where can you be a mentor? How can you be a foster parent? What can you do to help clean up the neighborhood or parks and make these areas welcoming for kids to play? Are you willing to paint or do a home makeover? Stop and take a moment to write down your top three ideas regarding service to the local community.

The Second C - Global Community

The ability to travel halfway around the world or to communicate through the internet has made the world a much smaller place. The news and its ability to cover stories from all over the world show us the challenges that others face. Some people are moved to contribute to others in need financially. Others are willing to go and help physically. Like the last section (local community), this section deals with the human need for connection and contribution.

I'll give you a great example. The Prison Education Project (PEP) started in 2011 with the idea of reducing the high recidivism rate in California. PEP's goal is to enhance the educational opportunities and experiences of those incarcerated to better prepare them for when they are released. PEP empowers the imprisoned to see more opportunities in front of them which reduces the chances to recidivate. PEP began with a focus on making an impact on the local community.

However, the issue of reducing recidivism is a concern anywhere there are incarcerated people. When Professor Arthur SSerwanga in Uganda wanted to create a program to enhance the educational opportunities for those incarcerated in preparation for their release, the internet directed him to the

PEP. He contacted PEP, and PEP Uganda was born. Over the last few years, volunteers have traveled to the country of Uganda and provided various curricula such as dance, yoga, entrepreneurship and several other classes. An idea that was born to assist the local community became one affecting the global community.

What ways can you impact the global community? I invite you to think of three ideas you feel that could positively impact both your local and global communities. This invitation might stretch your imagination like never before. Maybe you believe that just being able to get through each day and take care of your immediate needs is more than enough to bear. However, I challenge you to realize your struggle is often the struggle of the person next to you (in one form or another) as well as the person who is across the world. As you create ideas that will change your life and your local community, these same ideas may impact somebody that is part of the global "family."

Stop and write down your three ideas to positively impact the global community.

Chapter 6
Goals (Step 2)

"It always seems impossible until it's done."
-**Nelson Mandela**

What exactly are goals and why should we set them? One way to define goals is goals are merely your specific dreams with a timeline. When you put a timeframe on your dreams, it gives you something concrete to aim for and a deadline to attain it. Imagine being in a room and you have to hit a target. You're blindfolded, spun around and you have no idea where the target is. What are your chances of hitting that target? Probably slim to none. Goals are the same way. Most people have dreams that are not specific or do not have a "target" date. Life is constantly pulling us in different directions, but goals refocus us on our "targets."

For example, do you have a dream car? Do you know the exact specifications of it? Some of the specifications you want to know are: auto maker, model, year, exterior color, interior color, tires, seat material, transmission, etc. Once you have all the details you desire, you then need to do your research to find out how much it is going to cost. Let's say your car will cost you $48,000. Once you know the cost, you have a specific financial target. You then need to set a specific date to have the $48,000, so you can get your dream car. Let's say you set your goal to get that car in two years. You have now set your financial and timeline goals.

S.M.A.R.T Goals

When setting your goals, I invite you to set S.M.A.R.T. goals. What are S.M.A.R.T. goals? The acronym stands for:

"S" is for Specific. Be specific about what you want.

"M" is for Measurable. Can you measure if you are making progress towards or away from your goals?

"A" is for Attainable. Something you can get.

"R" stands for relevant and relatable to your overall goals. If you set a goal that isn't related to your total dream, then it can be a waste of time.

"T" stands for timely. Setting a time limit for achieving the goal is going to compel you into action. If you set the time for attainment too far off in the future, it may not give you the drive, urgency, or focus on accomplishing that goal.

Impossible Versus Improbable

"Unreasonable people rule the world."
George Bernard Shaw.

When you look at the people you identify as successful, at some point they had to be unreasonable in the way that they studied, trained or pursued what was thought of as impossible goals, especially for the individual.

I want to acknowledge the fact that as you begin or continue to pursue your goals, you will have to strike a precise balance between pursuing the "impossible" (something you may have control over) versus the improbable (something you have no power over).

One great example of a goal that was considered humanly impossible was running a mile in less than four minutes until Sir Roger Gilbert Bannister did it on May 6, 1954. Now, it's commonplace to see high school athletes run sub-four-minute miles. Just because a goal is impossible right now does not mean it shouldn't be pursued. In fact, progress happens when pursuing impossible goals. Much of modern technology was once thought to be impossible.

On the other hand, I define "improbable" as something that you have no control over. Improbable goals cause you to

56

beat your head against the wall trying to achieve something that may not be achievable. For example, trying to gain someone's approval or acceptance of what you want to do and who you are may not be possible because no matter what you do, you will never gain their approval. Constantly I'm reminded of the saying "No prophet is accepted in his hometown" (Luke 4:24, *The Bible*, New International Version). Another one is "familiarity breeds contempt" (Aesop, *Aesop's Fables*, "The Fox and The Lion") when it comes to the idea of pursuing others' approval or acceptance. So be cautious when pursuing improbable goals that can ultimately make you feel defeated.

Now that we have defined how to set S.M.A.R.T goals, review the goals you have set in the previous chapter (Five F's and Two C's) and consider whether they may be impossible or improbable. Knowing the difference can save you a lot of wasted effort, energy, and heartache.

Chapter 7

The Plan (Step 3)

"A goal without a plan is just a wish."
-Antoine de Saint-Exupéry

Now that you have "peeled back the onion" and set S.M.A.R.T. goals, the question is what are you going to do to achieve your goals? The "what" is the plan! What is the difference between a plan and a goal? Imagine your life is a movie plot (just go with me on this one!), and there are five questions you have to answer before you get started.

Who? You!

What? Your "plan" to achieve your dreams/purpose.

Where? Here and now!

When? Goals set the timeline.

Why? Dreams are where fulfillment and purpose connect deeply to values and needs.

Now that you have the "movie plot" questions answered, all that is left to do is to get the clapperboard and say . . . . Action!

The following is a scenario of how I take a goal and devise a plan. I live in California and suppose I have a beloved relative who is terminally ill in New York. It is important to me to share my appreciation in person for all of the ways the relationship has benefited me and has made me a better human being! Connection with family is central to my dreams. Therefore, I have a desire of expressing my appreciation in person. I then set a goal to do it and travel in the next thirty days. Will it be by a car, plane, train or foot? How much money will I need? Where will I stay? What will I bring? How long will I stay? When do I have to get back? All of the answers to those questions are parts of the plan. The plan is the execution of goals.

Blending Goals into a Plan

Having a successful life plan means your goals should not be conflicting but instead complementary to each other. For example, for my faith goals, I want to spend more time in worship, meditation, reading, and fellowship. My family goals are focused on spending quality time with my son, wife, and friends. My financial goals include reducing debt and increasing net worth. My fitness goals have me running 5K weekly and a 10K monthly. Lastly, my fun goals consist of a lot of travel! These goals should be all blended into my Life Success Plan. So what would be the plan? I planned to become an entrepreneur so I could use my time the way I wanted to rather than somebody else dictating my schedule. Presently, I can cut and paste my time. For example, the perfect day starts with spending time with my son and wife, working in the afternoon, and in the evening, gathering with other for prayer, fellowship, reading, and meditation. Each of those categories (faith, family, and finance) have individual goals, but the overall plan that combines these goals is the Life Success Plan.

How are you going to achieve your goals? How are you going to make money if you need it to realize your goals? Usually, most people make money through their chosen careers or professions. When people think of careers, they think of titles (engineer, lawyer, doctor, etc.) first. I invite you first to consider the activities you love to do, then search for the career titles that match them. Some of the questions you need to ask yourself when contemplating your career or profession are:

- What are you good at?
- What do you like to do?
- What is it that you want to do?

The questions may look and sound the same, but the answers may be very different. For example, you may be "good" with paperwork, but you "like" to socialize and you "want" to run a business. The ideal situation might be to create a business around people socializing with minimal, if any, paperwork. If your answer to all three questions is the same, then picking a career is easy! When you do what you love, then you never work a day in your life! It won't just be about earning money. We all have to make money. The best way to earn money is by creating tremendous value. Money is the byproduct of the value you create. Value is the love (enthusiasm, attention, detail, etc.) you put into what you are doing and effectively communicating it to your target audience. Create value by loving your career, and the money should come. Hence, it is essential to choose your career based on what you love to do rather than solely on a title.

Inflexible Outcome, Flexible Approach

Stay inflexible about the outcome, but be flexible about the approach. What do I mean? Let's say you want to be a millionaire because your dreams and goals require you to be one to achieve them. You decide to be a neurosurgeon to gain that million dollars. Unfortunately, you cannot pass the exams to be a neurosurgeon. Once you realize your plan (the "how") to be a neurosurgeon is not going to happen, you decide to become an entrepreneur who opens medical offices for neurosurgeons because you understand what they need in an office environment. That change still allows you to achieve the million dollars you need for your goals. That change is an example of staying inflexible about the outcome but being flexible about the approach.

As you lay out your plan, one of the most significant questions you have to ask yourself is what are the behaviors you need to develop to achieve those plans? I believe one of the keys to having life success is taking and exercising control over your life's direction. If you are not satisfied or happy with where your life is today, you have to become the captain of your ship. You have to become your greatest cheerleader. You have to take bold, massive steps to change what you are getting by changing what you are doing. If you want to save more money than you are saving now, what would you need to do differently? What action steps would you take? What attitude would you have? Because if you did not have to change at all, then you would already have achieved your goals and executed your plans. Because you have not, you need to identify what behaviors and attitudes will help you accomplish those goals.

For example, if someone wants to be in better health, there would need to be a shift in their behaviors regarding nutrition. What ways could they modify what, when and how much they ate? Some other areas they would want to pay attention to are exercise, water intake and quality of sleep. Regarding exercise, what would be their plan? Would they join a gym or work out at home?

What is your plan that blends your clearly defined goals (the Five F's and Two C's)? Stop here and begin to write it down. Be patient with the process because it may take a while.

Chapter 8
Schedule (Step 4)

"You'll never change your life until you change something you do daily. The secret of your success is found in your daily routine."
-John C. Maxwell

When you hear the word schedule, what comes to mind? Do you feel stressed thinking about it or you can't live without it? Does it inspire you or demotivate you? Do you feel constricted by it or do you feel set free by it? It is imperative to understand precisely what the word "schedule" means to you because the success of your life plan is in the focused execution of your daily schedule.

Twenty-Four Hours in a Day

We all have twenty-four hours a day. When you think of people who are successful in life, realize they only have twenty-four hours in a day, just like you and me. Most people assume that those who are successful have no challenges. Every human being has difficulties, obstacles, and setbacks. Every human being has their unique problems. Ultimately, successful people are successful because of their daily discipline executing their schedule. When you look at your schedule, how do your month, week, day and quarter hour programs look? I honestly believe the order of the F's (Faith, Family, Finance, Fitness, and Fun) is a prioritizing list. However, this doesn't mean that the order of the list will stay this way in any given moment or any given day.

For example, although I believe faith is the number one priority, it can be superseded by another priority. If someone's child or family member is sick or in danger, then they must prioritize family time. They may miss opportunities to fellowship or meditate, or they may have to adjust those areas to make sure their family gets well or is safe. If their business is suffering, they may need to focus, work overtime and push to get it back on track. If they have a job that requires overtime because there is a particular project to finish, then finance (work/income) becomes the priority.

Given that at any moment priorities can shift or change, you still want to have an idea of how you intend to use the twenty-four hours ahead of you. I propose the first question to answer is where in your daily schedule is your time for exercising your faith? Whether it is fellowshipping, visiting a particular place of worship, meditating, reading, etc., how is "faith time" showing up in your schedule? For example, maybe "faith time" is from 6 a.m. to 7 a.m. daily.

Now you can't schedule other goals in that time block.

The family may be next. Whether you have a family,
child or significant other, scheduling quality time for them is
vital. Make time for your family because if you don't, your
lack of attention will show up in negative displays for
attention. Where in your schedule is family time? Maybe
there is a family night or a date night with your significant
other that does not include children.

The next block of time might go to finance (generating
income). When are your income making hours? Some people
believe the first thing to get scheduled on a calendar is the
income making hours. They believe in prioritizing the income
making hours because the income provides the opportunity to
finance your ideal lifestyle.

Fitness is next. Good health is a cornerstone of real
wealth. What does your fitness regimen look like on a daily or
weekly basis?

The last, but not least, "F" to schedule is allocating
time blocks for fun. What are you going to do that you really
enjoy doing that is not an obligation? If you're not crystal
clear about what you enjoy doing, then review chapter five

and your notes to generate ideas for fun. I encourage you to look for daily opportunities to laugh hard and out loud!

Make time for Community, both locally and globally! Schedule time to get to know your local community better through participation in activities and talking to your neighbors! Find ways to bring value to local community events. Global events have real-world consequences in real-time. Become aware of opportunities to uplift and positively impact the global community.

Now that you have scheduled the five F's and the two C's, you will hopefully find that your week is filled up. You have allocated time to all the areas that are important.

If you have time blocks where there are overlapping goals, ask yourself what ways you can adjust some of the overlaps. If you move something out of one place in your schedule, make sure it shows up somewhere else.

For example, if I'm suddenly requested to attend a meeting next week that will take time away from my family, fitness or faith goals, I intend on putting those displaced goals somewhere else in my schedule. I'm continually reflecting on where I can make adjustments (course correction), so I can still achieve all of my daily and weekly goals.

Scheduling Everything

I recall the first time I sincerely understood prioritizing a schedule was when I was at a business meeting where a couple was speaking about how they were becoming more successful by mastering their schedule. At one point they were struggling financially, martially, and in other areas of their lives. They talked about scheduling everything, including time for intimacy! Weekly, they planned a date night, so there was time to connect even during their most hectic times.

I remember being taken aback hearing what they were saying. I thought, "What do you mean you schedule your intimacy time and date night; don't you just make it up as you go along?" That seemed so unspontaneous and robotic!

I observed this couple over the next few years, and this is what I noticed:

- Their income multiplied many times over.
- Their family grew.
- Their faith and marital relationship deepened.
- The impact they were able to have on others and help others dramatically grow increased.

I took a brutally candid look at my life through my schedule. I realized I made it up as I went along and that was not working at all. I found that my life often looked like those acrobats who have the spinning plate on top of the thin pole. They spin the plate and then get another plate on another pole and spin it and so on. Pretty soon the first plate starts to wobble, and they would run back to the first plate and get it spinning steadily again. The goal was to see how many plates they can get to rotate on the poles without the plates falling and breaking. Eventually, some of them would fall and break. The great acrobats were able to keep dozens of plates spinning, but the average acrobat would have plates fall and break. This concept of spinning plates was another critical point in helping me understand focus, discipline and not having too many plates spinning in the air at the same time.

Crystal Balls versus Rubber Balls

Another principle is knowing the difference between which items are "crystal balls" and which ones are "rubber balls." A crystal ball, if dropped, will break into sharp pieces with little chances of recovery. A rubber ball, however, will bounce back (recovery). For example, if I miss too many date nights with my wife, eventually that will show up as dissatisfaction and strain on the relationship because we are not connecting or on the same page. That becomes a crystal ball. If there is a legitimate reason why I reschedule date night and follow up, that becomes a rubber ball because there's an opportunity to recover the missed opportunity.

If you believe you'll find life success in your daily schedule, how can you maximize the twenty-four hours in a day that you have? How can you reduce your distractions? I highly recommend that you have a calendar that allows you to schedule your day in fifteen-minute increments.

Stop and review your schedule for the next three days (72 hours). Some things to think about are:

- Is your sleep time planned (part of Fitness)?
- Any of the five F's and two C' missing?
- Any changes you want to make?

Chapter 9
Accountability (Step 5)

"Accountability breeds response-ability."
-Stephen R. Covey

Accountability has become a word that is disliked, feared and even dreaded by many. Those who loathe it compare any accountability to a stressful work evaluation assessing performance, often by someone they may not like or even respect. Those same individuals dread responsibility in many areas of their life. If that is your view, I am going to invite you to shift your perspective of the process of accountability.

Accountability: Self or Coach?

Accountability merely is a measuring tool that allows you to assess if you are on or off track towards achieving your goals.

A person can be accountable in a couple of ways, mostly by being held accountable by someone else (what I like to call an "accountability coach") or self-accountability using an accountability system. The question you have to answer is, what system will you use? Both systems are great. Which one you choose will depend on what will inspire you to take action - either an accountability coach or self-accountability - to transform. If you notice that you are most motivated to take action when someone else is "coaching" you, then you will benefit from having an accountability coach. If you take action from self-inspiration, then self-accountability is right for you.

If the idea of an accountability coach sounds inspiring, some of the criteria for an accountability coach are, but are not limited to, someone who:

- You hold in high esteem or respect.
- Can challenge you to get out of your "comfort zone" and get back on track.
- Can be entirely, and sometimes brutally, honest with you and vice versa.
- Can motivate and inspire you while also giving you intense constructive criticism.

Self-accountability best suits you if you can keep your word to yourself, do exactly what you say and don't need anyone to remind you of what you need to do.

Many authors have provided accountability systems by which others can benefit. Some of these systems are in CDS, DVDs, websites, books, memoirs or autobiographies like Legendary Coach John Wooden's *Pyramid of Success*.

For example, Napoleon Hill wrote the business and personal development classic *Think and Grow Rich*. He shared his summation of hundreds of interviews with successful people and how they stay focused and disciplined while pursuing their dreams. The book talks about setting up a plan, being very specific about exactly what you want and what you are willing to do or give for it. Once you have the plan, you must write it down and read it at least twice a day (in the morning upon awakening and at night before laying down to sleep). Read it more if the opportunity arises. He has been deceased for many years, but the system he left behind for self-accountability still brings incredible value to many!

As you begin to measure your progress, it will be crucial to know your "baseline" or starting point. One method of measuring your baseline is using the "scale of 1-10". On a scale of 1-10, with 1 being desperately needing massive improvement and 10 being superbly excellent, how would you rate yourself right now in each of the Five F's and the Two C's? Each rating is your baseline for that subject. Decide how often you will measure yourself in each area to identify if you are growing or not. Rating yourself once every other week is a good starting point. The ultimate goal is not to be a perfect 10 in every category. No one is. Some categories, if you even improve from a two to a four, will show that you have made considerable developments in your transformation!

Whether you have an accountability coach or choose self-accountability, it must be clear that ultimately there are only a couple of things you can control. **The two main things you can control are your attitude and your actions.** Your "altitude" (how far you go regarding personal growth and success) is based mainly on your attitude. What do I mean by attitude? How you feel and think about your current circumstances, prospects, challenges, talents, other people and the world around you comprise your attitude. Your attitude reflects how you view and behave towards events that happen. Do you see events happening *to* you (harmful) or *for* you (ultimate benefit)? How you give meaning to the circumstances and situations in your life will reflect your attitude. Your accountability system becomes a critical assessment of your attitude. Are you open to constructive criticism to help you build the foundation and structure you need to achieve your dreams or do you resent it?

A substantial question to persistently ask yourself is, "What can I learn from this?" There are no perfect questions or statements for every single moment; however, I found this one to be great. I discovered that when I ask myself this question, whether a setback or a fantastic victory has happened, my mind is more open to receiving the value of what can be a marvelous teaching moment.

Impact of Environment, Internal & External Influences

One aspect of accountability and behavior assessment is a profound awareness of the impact of three things: the environment around us, internal influences that drive us and external influences that guide us. I define the environment, internal influences, and external influences as follows:

- Environment is the living associations of your community (family, friends, coworkers, etc.)
- Internal influence comprises of one's core beliefs which affect thoughts and emotions.
- External influences are what one adheres to regarding societal, familial and economic structures and traditions.

It is imperative to pay close attention to your
environment, internal and external influences because your
attitude, behavior and so much more is the sum of the five
people with whom you spend the most time. Internal
influence is one's core beliefs which affect thoughts and
emotions. Where you are right now in all areas of your life is
often the sum of those five people. Study their actions and
behaviors. Are those the actions and behaviors you need to do
or have to achieve your definition of a successful life? Pay
even closer attention to how they express themselves in
casual, unexpected moments which reveal their real attitudes.
Are those the attitudes you want to possess, and will they help
you accomplish your goals? Take a moment and think about
those five people with whom you spend the most time. Ask
yourself: do I want their life or lifestyle? Do they seem
fulfilled, excited, content and happy with their own life? If
not, then you may need to change your associations.

Is it possible to change those associations? Yes! Will
it be easy? It depends. Some people feel if they change
associations that means that they have to forget where they
came from or that they have "sold out." Life isn't about
forgetting where you came from, but being present and
focusing on where you are going. There will need to be some

76

major changes to achieve your goals. You may have to exercise more, eat better, sleep better, read more, travel more, etc. You have to be willing to change or let go of any associations that are holding you back from pursuing your dreams! While you change associations, you have to constantly remind yourself that you are choosing to pursue a different life than the one you have lived. You can't get into shape if you hang out with people who are not trying to get into shape. You can't get rid of habits if you hang around people who indulge in those particular habits. Insanity is doing the same thing over and over again and expecting a different result. It won't happen unless you make it happen!

Your environment can be stronger than your will. Pay close attention to the environments you find yourself in. Often those who are the closest to us are the ones who can unintentionally or intentionally prevent us from actualizing or pursuing our dreams. Some people will inadvertently discourage you by what they say and do (or what they don't say and do). They may be very sincere and not want to see you get hurt or suffer. Others intentionally put you and your efforts down because your transformation may make them feel uncomfortable. Looking within themselves, they may realize they are not willing to get out of their comfort zone and put in the work of transformation in pursuing their dreams. They may encourage you to be safe and stay within your comfort zone, but the best-lived life is the one lived outside of your comfort zone! The most fabulous rewards in life often come with taking the most significant risks: asking someone to marry you, having a baby, quitting a job, etc. If you truly embrace the fact that there are no failures, just lessons, then risks are worthwhile if you are pursuing your dreams.

Since your core beliefs comprise your internal influence which affects your thoughts and emotions, being aware of what your core beliefs are is crucial to your success. There's debate about whether or not thoughts affect emotions or emotions affect thoughts, but both of these arguments focus on your core beliefs. What are your core beliefs? Do you believe the universe and everything that happens is collaborating with you or conspiring against you? When you look at what your core beliefs are, where did they originate? There is a story of a traditional family who served a roast, every holiday. They would cut a section of it off before serving it. One of the young, adult women in this family planned to carry on the tradition and wanted to know why they cut off the end of the roast. So she asked her mom. Her mom said, "I don't know; your grandma always did that." The young girl went to her grandma and asked, "Why is the end of the roast always cut off?" The grandma answered, "Because it couldn't fit into the pan." This custom was passed down generationally and replicated without being questioned. When you look at your core beliefs about the world, yourself, what you deserve and who you are, where did they come from initially?

Did you know you can change your core beliefs? Some of them you can change overnight while others you will need to work on diligently but know that you can change your beliefs. The question you need to ask yourself is, are your current core beliefs serving you to get closer to your dreams or are they taking you further away from them?

External influences come from outside of you. They may come from what people have said. Did someone ever tell you that you would never win in life? That you are not worthy of the best things this life has to offer? If you believed them, then that can become your core belief about yourself. However, does the fact they said it, makes it true? What if you choose to reject what they said because you realize it is not serving you to evolve into the person you wish to be? What if you decide to say, "I reject those particular beliefs"? What if you take on the new beliefs that you do deserve the best that life has to offer and that you have the right and privilege to pursue it?

If your core beliefs affect your thoughts and emotions, which then affect your actions and ultimately your results, would you agree being aware of them and shaping them to benefit you is vital? If you want different results, then you have to take different actions based on new thoughts, emotions and core beliefs. How do you shift your core beliefs? You may need to change some of your associations, read more books, listen to CDs, attend seminars, etc. Your actions, behaviors, and attitude will then reflect the person who you need to be to achieve your goals.

Stop and write down the answers to the following questions to make this chapter the most productive:

1. Who are the five people with whom you spend the most time?
    a. What are their top 3-5 behaviors?
    b. What are 3-5 statements that reflect their current attitude and behaviors?

2. What is or what will be your accountability system? Do you/will you have an accountability coach or are you choosing to be self-accountable?

3. Why will your accountability system keep your "feet to the fire" of the transformation of what your dreams, goals, plan, and schedule need to be?

Chapter 10

The Secret Ingredient

"What strikes me is that there's a very fine line between success and failure. Just one ingredient can make the difference."
-Andrew Lloyd Webber

Now that you have read this book, you may be asking yourself what is the "secret ingredient" to successfully making this Life Success Plan work? My answer is there is no secret ingredient! There's only putting in the work! Anyone that you regard as successful has put in the work. My greatest hope is that you accept the invitation inherently implied in this book:

Increase your self-awareness
and self-mastery through deep
introspection to live a
successful life according to your
definition.

I invite you to put in the work! It is going to require you to make changes for you to transform into the person you want and need to be. If you could stay the same person and get the results in your life you really want deep down inside, you would already have them! It is in the invitation, the challenge and the struggle you will grow most.

Consistency breeds success. Success is found in your daily schedule by how consistent you are in not getting distracted. Ultimately, your dreams are a wish your heart makes, and that wish can come true! How often you read this book, review your Life Success Plan and stay focused on your dreams is entirely up to you.

You are going to take your next breath and, eventually, you are going to take your last. In between those two, what will matter most will not be the things you will amass; it will be how you lived and it mattered to others that you lived. Did you leave everything on the table and hold nothing back regarding your unique talents, gifts, and value or did you die with them still inside you? Did you impact people's lives and make a difference while you were here?

At the end of the day, your dreams and goals should make you experience fulfillment in the life you live, appreciation for the things you have, contentment with having enough (whatever that might be) and gratitude for the people you choose to have around you. That is my definition of success. Being around who you want, doing what you want to do and when you want to do it.

If there is a significant takeaway I would want you to have, it would be the crucial part of the process of success is to enjoy the journey. All of it! You will appreciate much of it in hindsight, but I invite you to embrace all of it: the ups and the downs, the highs and the lows. It is in the downs and the lows that much of the growth in character, wisdom, and experience will happen. Naturally, while you are in them, they are not fun. They may be very painful and even heartbreaking. I encourage you to believe that what does not kill you can make you stronger. Be patient with the process of life and remember that "this too, shall pass." On the other side of the valleys of setbacks and low points will be peaks of strength and resolve you did not have before that will not only sustain you but drive you in pursuing your dreams!

Whether you achieve specific goals or dreams, the journey is what life success is all about! When you think of movies, what are some that have the most far-reaching success stories? It is the story of the underdog, the one who went up against insurmountable odds or unreasonable challenges and prevailed. Usually, the underdog did not want to be the hero, or he or she tried to run away from having to take on responsibility or be challenged to grow in a certain way. But when faced with no other choice, the underdog rose up to the challenge, made changes, grew and became triumphant. If you study these movies, you will see that growth happens in the journey.

Experience can be your most impressive teacher and your greatest asset. I challenge you to view "failure" as experience disguised as an opportunity to learn an invaluable lesson. You should even thank the people that gave you a hard time. Understand that they play a role in your growth.

Ultimately, success is found in the journey and not solely in the destination.

Hopefully, this book, the questions and the ideas shared are helpful in guiding you to live the best life possible with little regret and much fulfillment. If that has happened or that will happen, then I've done my job and congratulate you on the journey!

Take care!

Chapter 11
The Interview

Now that you have read this book, I thought it might be worthwhile for you to get to know more about me. I have included an interview I did in 2015 for the internet magazine *Juicy Highlights* entitled, "I Had Lost Faith, As My Life Turned Out Differently Than I Expected," which appeared in their "Believe and Inspire" section. The interview chronicles the "dots" of my life story from the downward spiral driven by fear leading to incarceration and the uplifting power of redemption, hope, and real unconditional Love. This interview captures the essence of my transformation from where I started to where I am now as an international inspirational speaker, moderator, and facilitator. I felt it was worthwhile to share that I write from personal experience in the transformative power for the concepts and content of this book.

I Had Lost Faith, As My Life Turned Out Differently Than I Expected

By Stephanie Gergeres

Requesting an interview with Mr. Fenelon was a fear that I was battling with because I had to get to a place of openness and understanding of people without judgment. Although, as human beings, we constantly judge a book by its cover, I had to decide for myself to let go of my thoughts to truly see the change Ernst has undergone to help and influence others, to be able to publish this story.

In proceeding with this interview, I realized that one of the components in life that many people don't recognize that shape their decisions throughout their daily lives is the "fear to lose it all." Many continue to struggle with their challenges and fears while others like Ernst, have found a way to step out on faith and consciously do the work that is needed to overcome his fears of being judged in many ways. Being able to witness and feel, his freedom to help others through his trials and tribulations, I have decided not to delve into details of his incarceration, because at the end of it all, what really matters is the future and how one person is recognizing their worth one by one, because of Mr. Fenelon. His story has definitely inspired me and many people in his community, which is why I wanted to share his story and inspiration that I felt as I was interviewing Mr. Fenelon.

JH: *What was your story that actually got you to the path of where you are in life?*

EF: *Shortly after my father died in 1988, two things happened. I began to decline into a serious depression and I met a woman with a young child with whom I would start what would be a 2 ½ year relationship. The relationship was very rocky at a time when I needed strength and stability. Ultimately the relationship ended badly and I took actions that I have remorse for and regret which lead to my incarceration.*

Sometimes in life, you don't realize what you have until it is taken away from you. That was me. I didn't appreciate how blessed I was in life. I only focused on my challenges and problems until I could think of nothing else. It was only when the truly precious things in life (family and friends who love you, health, freedom, being alive; etc.) were taken or in serious jeopardy that I realized how much they meant to me.

When I was at my lowest, someone shared a proverb which said: "The man with no shoes stopped complaining when he met the man with no feet." It stuck with me and reminded me things could be worse. I was at least alive and

*had a chance to live. I began regaining my humanity at that
point and have continued on that journey.*

JH: **How did you gather the pieces of your life to
start over?**

EF: *It wasn't easy, but I started with restoring my
faith and my relationship with Almighty God. I had lost faith
as my life turned out different than I expected.*

*Probably the biggest event that made me lose faith
and hope was my father's death. After battling cancer and
related health issues for 10 years, it became clear my father
was dying. I was raised believing at some point that if one
pleads with Almighty God, and prays fervently, He would
answer their prayers. If He didn't then it meant they didn't
"deserve" to have their prayers answered and He had turned
His back to them. I thought that I could "bargain" with The
Almighty. I prayed and he still died, so I thought The
Almighty had given up on my family and me. So I gave up on
The Almighty. As my life spiraled downwardly out of control,
eventually I found myself about to lose everything, including
my life.*

*It was in a moment of complete solitude from
everything and everyone I valued that I felt a presence that I*

call The Almighty. The spiritual conversation went something like Almighty God saying to me: "I never left. I have been here right beside you the whole time and always will be. I love you no matter what you said or did. It's not your time". I began to believe again that Almighty God's plan for my life has positive purpose. I began to reconnect through prayers of remorse, seeking mercy and forgiveness. My spiritual journey led me to accept Islam and become Muslim.

I came to accept the philosophy that "actor" and "act(s)" are separate. Therefore the "act" (my aberrant behavior) can be condemned without condemning the "actor" (me). This was an important self-concept in the process of healing, self-forgiveness and remorse for injuring others. I participated in several individual and group therapy sessions designed to give me tools to cope and heal my mind, heart and soul.

I became open again to receive the tremendous love, support and prayers of family and real friends. I then reached out to family and friends and apologized for my behavior and for any hurt I caused them.

I focused on what I could learn to contribute to society and create a livelihood. I renewed my studies of computer programs, but started studying business and constitutional law. I found I had a talent for law and developed a career as a law clerk/secretary. Eventually I left law and pursued a life dream of becoming an entrepreneur.

Lastly, I wanted to help those who needed help. I appreciated so much those who helped me when I needed it. I wanted to do the same for others. This led to my decision to work in hospice and other opportunities to help others. Even if it is just a smile.

JH: *What inspired you to want better for yourself and life?*

EF: *My restored faith in Almighty God's (Allah) love for me is first. My family/friends spiritual faith was important too. Their love for me and their unwavering belief that I am by nature a good person was critical. The history of my parents leaving Haiti to come to the USA to have a better life for me played a role too.*

For me, inspired means to operate from the "Spirit" with an outwardly focus of Love. Ultimately, my Spirit, under the correct influences and outward focus, wants everyone to be joyful.

My spirit looks for opportunities to improve or make things better to achieve that goal. When I became inwardly focused on my problems, I became selfish and self-centered.

I lost inspiration and began to operate in satisfying the flesh and mind. I discovered both are insatiable and any joy or happiness obtained through pure selfishness is temporary. At the end of the day, I find it most fulfilling when I connect and contribute with/to others.

JH: What transitions and/or steps did you take to realize this is the way I will give back?

EF: *I believe it was a progression of small steps with some quantum leaps in between. First, I had to help myself by working on being independent as much as possible. I had to learn to take complete care of myself without complete reliance on others. I had to learn to forgive and love myself first before I could really love others.*

I started "giving back" to others by helping out wherever I could. I would look for opportunities to be an extra hand. I would volunteer for cleanup after parties or events. I would take the unpopular opportunities that others passed up. I gave money in the form of religious duty ("tithes" while under Christianity and "Zakat" under Islam), but I

*began to believe that wasn't enough. One day one of my
mentors invited me to participate in an "extreme home
makeover" of an elderly woman in his community. Her
property had fallen into a state of decay. I participated and it
changed my life!*

*I then looked for opportunities in business that would
empower others. I loved the environment and principles of
World Financial Group (WFG) with its ability to have a great
self-empowerment program with a great compensation
package! I met my wife who had already been with WFG for
years and together we are building a great company by
building great people. I also liked the similar self-
improvement concepts of* <u>Melaleuca</u>*, the wellness company,
where I am building a business empire by building people up
as well.*

JH: **With giving back, what made you begin to
start working as a program coordinator at PEP?**

EF: *When the opportunity to go into prisons and
talk to and inspire inmates was first presented to me, I
declined it. I thought that I was too busy getting my life
together and honestly was freaked out with the prospect of
going through the doors of a prison. I was sure that I would*

not get approved, based on the negative comments of others. Also, I didn't think I had something to share that would make a difference to the lives of those incarcerated. Then I had a crisis in my life that turned my world upside down and challenged my perspective on everything. At the same time, the Prison Education Project (PEP) was about to have its initial session. Thankfully, my mentor Dr. Renford Reese, Ph.D. Challenged me by asking what I have to lose by applying, if approved, sharing my story, which he felt was inspirational. I am so thankful for his persistence and belief in me. I applied, was approved and the rest is history.

This one leap of faith has changed my life and that of many others. For me, with my entire life in turmoil, it gave me personal direction and purpose. I found out that my life and how I have overcome challenges is very motivational and inspirational for many.

JH: **How do you feel that this position has made a positive influence on others?**

EF: *My position as Program Coordinator proves that anything is possible and that unchallenged limitations cannot be broken or changed. I have been on panels, groups and gatherings for local and global perspectives on rehabilitation. I have spoken to dozens upon dozens of college*

*students about restorative justice and the meaning of
rehabilitation. I have traveled to Uganda and spoken to
hundreds of maximum security inmates and inspired them to
be better, and not bitter. I have had numerous inmates tell me
they are inspired to transform their lives. I even had one
inmate tell me that he changed his mind from committing
suicide because I cared to continue to show up and care. I
was told none of these things would ever happen but because
I challenged those limitations, they changed!*

JH: **How do you see that your work is your
calling?**

EF: *I believe that everything happens for a reason.
To be able to take personal tragedy and turn it into triumph is
amazing. I thought at first that my incarceration was just a
waste, but now I think differently. It started from the point
that I embraced my past as just that, my past.*

*What makes it powerful is who I became through the
process and since then. I became better and not bitter because
I found blessings in the intangible things of life: being alive,
being positive and helping others.*

*My current business and work is an extension of who I
am. It could be said that my motto could be the following:*

"To love those that are easy to hate, to help those it is easy not to want to help and to care about those some would want to forget". I am not a saint. Just a human being that works every day to see the humanity and spiritually in everyone, including myself.

JH: **Along with you being a program coordinator for PEP, how have you correlated that to also becoming a business entrepreneur?**

EF: *I was taught that to be a true entrepreneur, I had to understand that I am in the "people" business. What that means to me is that my business is understanding the wants and need of people, their thoughts and behaviors. I am not in the business of the product or service I am offering.*

The same can be said of the PEP Program Coordinator position; it is my "business" to understand the minds and hearts of the inmates, staff and students. Our purpose is the transformation of preconceptions, perceptions and biases of others in the pursuit of the realization that we are all connected through the human spirit regardless of social status and position. I treat the program and its challenges like a business, bringing professionalism and diplomacy in addressing issues and concerns.

JH: *What would be your advice to others who have been in your position?*

EF: *The first step is to pensively reflect and take personal accountability and responsibility for one's actions and attitude. I have come to believe that each individual is ultimately responsible for only two things in the universe: their actions and attitude. I encourage people to become aware of what are the influences in their life that affect their thoughts and actions. I deeply encourage people to get out of the "Blame Game" as quickly as possible. No one else is responsible for their happiness. Blaming gives away power. Accepting responsibility gives power. The power to change simply by making a real decision and acting upon it.*

One must take time to properly nourish the mind, body and soul/spirit. The soul/spirit is nourished by prayer and/or meditation and connection. The mind is nourished by the ideals and thoughts it consumes. Consume positive thoughts and ideas and it begins producing positive thoughts and ideas, which in turn produce positive actions. The body is nourished by proper intake of water, nutritional foods, exercise and rest. Lastly, I advise to look at one's associations (positive associations encourage positive actions, etc.) and get a mentor who will always inspire positive growth and critical thinking in pursuit of one's positive goals.

JH: **What is one important life lesson you have learned, that you feel that you can pass on to others?**

EF: *I had the opportunity and privilege to work in a hospice for a few years. The Life lesson I learned is "Life is too short to get to your death bed and realize that you haven't really lived." I learned that I don't want to spend a lot of energy arguing over issues (sports, religion, politics, etc.) that won't matter when I am about to die. It's critical to get crystal clear on what is really important to you. Some questions that have helped me get crystal clear is: Who do you love? Why do you love them? What do you want to do for them and leave behind for them? Get Crystal Clear and truly live!*

JH: **What is a quote that you live by on an everyday basis?**

EF: *"Be the change you wish to see in the world."- Mahatma Gandhi*

18 Great Reads on Transformation of Mindset and Soul

Autobiography of Malcolm X by Malcolm X

Rich Dad Poor Dad by Robert Kiyosaki

Cashflow Quadrant by Robert Kiyosaki

Seven Habits of Highly Effective People by Stephen Covey

Who Moved My Cheese by Spencer Johnson

The Art of War by Sun Tzu

The Five Rings by Miyamoto Musashi

The Richest Man in Babylon by George S. Clason

The Speed of Trust by Stephen M. R. Covey

The Power of Intention by Dr. Wayne W. Dyer

Secrets of the Millionaire Mind by T. Harv Eker

The Art of Seduction by Robert Greene

The 48 Laws of Power by Robert Greene

Manifesting for Non Gurus by Robert MacPhee

The Four Agreements by Don Miguel Ruiz

177 Mental Toughness Secrets of the World Class by Steve Siebold

A New Earth by Eckhart Tolle

The Power of Now by Eckhart Tolle

About the Author

Born in Brooklyn, New York, Ernst Fenelon Jr.
learned early in life to have deep empathy and compassion for
people, especially those less fortunate in society. He learned
these and other principles at the knees of his Haitian parents,
who immigrated to the United States after receiving political
asylum. Those learned principles continue to be his guiding
force today.

Ernst has spoken on local, national and international
platforms about rehabilitation and prison reform efforts. He
provides a unique perspective on the United States prison
education, reintegration and rehabilitation discussions with 25
years of experience with the California prison system,
including formerly being incarcerated himself.

He has been interviewed on Radio (*NPR*), TV (*Al-
Jazeera America*), Several podcasts (*Youth Matters, Middle
Ground and Show Talk with Angela Butler*), and in
Newspapers (including *Pasadena Now).*

Ernst is the Senior Program Coordinator for The Prison Education Project (PEP) (www.prisoneducationproject.org), Program Coordinator for the PEP-Uganda program (www.pepuganda.org), a facilitator for the "Trust Talks" (www.trusttalks.org) and the current Moderator for the YWCA Pasadena "Talking the Talk" series (www.ywca.org). His current work with these and other organizations is designed to bring hope to individuals and create environments for opposing parties willing to be open to seek solutions to their pressing issues.

Ernst is an inspirational public speaker and transformational coach who has encouraged people around the world to lead a more positive and productive life by sharing his paradoxical life experiences and presenting his solution-based perspective.

Ernst's philosophy is *"Every Problem has a solution, and every solution begins with having a conversation. I believe life has positioned me to have a unique perspective to start the conversation. So let's start the conversation."*

For more information, booking for speaking engagements or personal/organizational coaching sessions, go to: www.ernstfenelonjr.com.